MEERKATS
WORK TOGETHER

ELLIOT MONROE

New York

Published in 2018 by The Rosen Publishing Group, Inc.
29 East 21st Street, New York, NY 10010

First Edition

Editor: Melissa Raé Shofner
Book Design: Michael J. Flynn

Photo Credits: Cover anetapics/Shutterstock.com; p. 4 Aaron Amat/Shutterstock.com; p. 5 Mrinal Pal/Shutterstock.com; p. 6 Nazzu/Shutterstock.com; p. 7 aaltair/Shutterstock.com; p. 8 lendy16/Shutterstock.com; p. 9 boreala/Shutterstock.com; p. 11 Nasared/Shutterstock.com; p. 13 David W. Macdonald/Oxford Scientific/Getty Images; p. 15 Kelsey Green/Shutterstock.com; p. 17 Barcroft/Barcroft Media/Getty Images; p. 19 aSuruwataRi/Shutterstock.com; pp. 20–21 Nigel Dennis/Gallo Images/Getty Images; p. 22 Will Burrard-Lucas/Nature Picture Library/Getty Images.

Cataloging-in-Publication Data

Names: Monroe, Elliot.
Title: Meerkats work together / Elliot Monroe.
Description: New York : PowerKids Press, 2018. | Series: Animal teamwork | Includes index.
Identifiers: ISBN 9781508155515 (pbk.) | ISBN 9781508155454 (library bound) | ISBN 9781508155331 (6 pack)
Subjects: LCSH: Meerkat–Juvenile literature. | Meerkat–Behavior–Juvenile literature.
Classification: LCC QL737.C235 M66 2018 | DDC 599.74'2–dc23

Manufactured in the United States of America

CPSIA Compliance Information: Batch #BS17PK: For Further Information contact Rosen Publishing, New York, New York at 1-800-237-9932

CONTENTS

MEET THE MEERKAT

What animals are small, furry, and ready to scurry in a hurry? Meerkats! These small desert animals depend on each other to stay safe. If a predator is nearby, they send out a warning and dart quickly underground.

Life in the desert isn't easy, but meerkats have several **adaptations** that help them survive. They live in large groups and are some of nature's best masters of teamwork. Meerkats work together to raise their young, build their homes, and keep their family safe.

MONGOOSE

CRITTER COOPERATION

Meerkats are also called suricates. They belong to the mongoose family.

A group of meerkats is called a gang, a clan, or a mob.

FUR, CLAWS, AND TAILS

Meerkats are small **mammals**. When fully grown, they stand around 12 inches (30.5 cm) tall and weigh about 2.2 pounds (1 kg). They have brown-striped fur. Meerkats have a pointed face. Darker fur grows around their eyes.

Meerkats have a long, skinny tail. When they stand tall on their back legs, their tail helps them balance, or stay upright without falling over. Meerkats are fast and can run up to 20 miles (32.2 km) per hour.

Meerkats have long claws to help them dig in the dirt to find food.

CRITTER COOPERATION

Unlike other members of the mongoose family, meerkats don't have a bushy tail.

DESERT LIFE

Meerkats live in southern Africa. They can be found in parts of Namibia, Botswana, South Africa, and southwestern Angola. They live in deserts and grasslands. A meerkat mob's territory is usually about 4 square miles (10.4 km sq). They mark this area with their scent.

Each day, meerkats move around their territory foraging, or looking for food, together. They have several **burrows** throughout their territory that they use for **protection** and sleeping. Burrows have multiple entrances, many tunnels, and several chambers, or rooms.

Meerkats often live in burrows dug by other animals, such as ground squirrels. Burrows keep meerkats safe and cool underground.

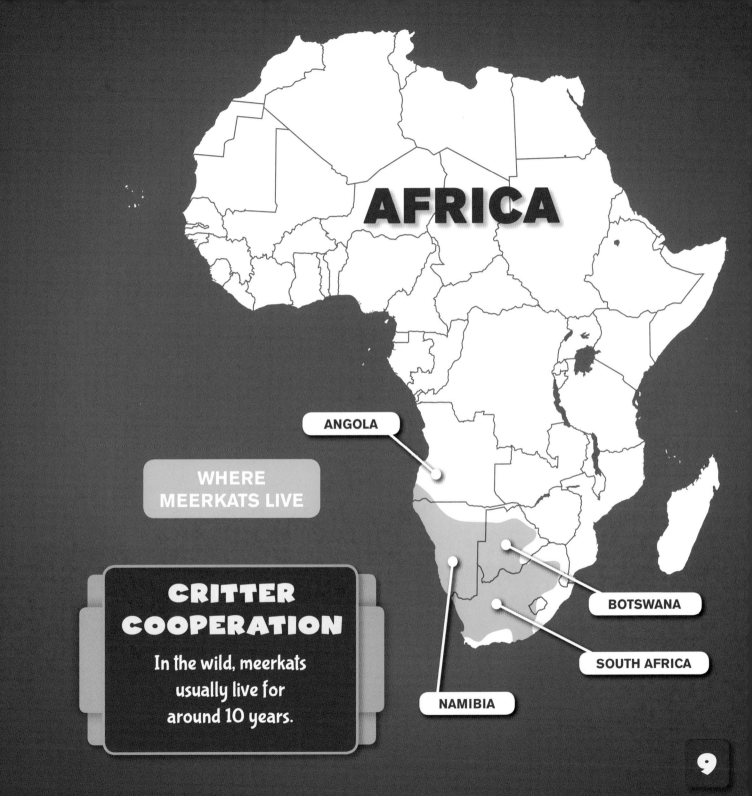

AFRICA

WHERE
MEERKATS LIVE

ANGOLA

BOTSWANA

SOUTH AFRICA

NAMIBIA

CRITTER COOPERATION

In the wild, meerkats usually live for around 10 years.

9

MEERKAT FAMILIES

A meerkat mob can be quite large. Some have between 30 and 50 members! There may be several meerkat families within a mob. Each mob has a **dominant** female leader. This female and a dominant male have most of the babies within the mob.

Meerkats are diurnal. This means they sleep at night and are awake during the day. Each morning, members of a meerkat family spend time cleaning each other's fur and sitting in the sun. The rest of the day is spent foraging together.

CRITTER COOPERATION

Meerkats are very social animals. Members of a mob get along with each other very well.

Meerkats like to lie in the sun to warm up. They lie on rocks, sit in the shade, or hide in their burrows to cool off.

SEARCHING FOR FOOD

Meerkats are omnivores. This means they eat plants and meat. They mainly eat insects, or bugs, that they find while digging in the dirt. Meerkats aren't picky eaters, though. They'll also eat fruit, plants, birds, small reptiles, eggs, and even other small mammals.

Meerkats don't have much body fat, which means they don't have much stored energy. They need to search for food every day to stay alive. They don't need to drink a lot of water, though. They get what they need from the foods they eat.

CRITTER COOPERATION

Baby meerkats learn how to kill and eat scorpions by watching adult meerkats. They learn in stages, starting with dead scorpions and working their way up to live ones.

Meerkats can hunt and eat scorpions! First, they move in fast and rip off the scorpion's **venomous** stinger. Then they wipe any remaining venom off the scorpion by rubbing it in the sand before chowing down.

13

CARING FOR PUPS

Baby meerkats are called pups. The dominant female has three to five babies at a time, usually during the rainy season when there's more food around. Pups are born underground in a burrow where they're safe from predators.

Meerkats work together to care for the young. Members of a mob take turns watching over the pups while their mother forages for food. Mob members teach pups how to survive in the desert. Pups spend much of their time playing with each other.

CRITTER COOPERATION

Meerkat pups can't see or hear and have almost no fur when they're born. By the time they're two months old, however, they look just like adults!

Baby meerkats leave their burrow for the first time when they're about four weeks old.

SPECIAL ADAPTATIONS

Meerkats have several adaptations that help them survive in the desert. They have excellent eyesight, with which they watch for danger to protect the mob. They also have a great sense of smell. This helps them find food.

Meerkats are built for digging. They have special **membranes** that keep dirt out of their eyes. They're also able to close their ears. These adaptations, along with their long, sharp claws, allow members of a mob to make easy work of foraging and digging burrows.

CRITTER COOPERATION

Meerkats can spot a bird in the sky from more than 984 feet (300 m) away. The dark fur around their eyes reduces **glare** so they can see better!

The desert can be unsafe, so meerkats are always on alert. Their fur helps them blend in with rocks and grasses in their **environment**.

MAKING NOISE

Meerkats communicate, or talk to each other, using many different sounds. Scientists think they use at least 10 different noises to communicate. If danger is nearby, meerkats bark, **whistle**, or make other loud warning noises. Meerkats may also **growl**, spit, or make quiet sounds called murmurs.

Young meerkats make peeping noises while they play. The more excited they are, the louder the sound. Sometimes, when they're happy, pups will purr like a cat.

CRITTER COOPERATION

Meerkats make different warning noises depending on whether they see a predator in the air or on land.

Female meerkats make noise more often than male meerkats.

ON THE LOOKOUT

To keep their group safe, meerkats take turns acting as a sentry, or guard. A sentry will climb to the highest point in the area, stand up tall, and keep an eye out for danger. If a sentry spots danger, it will make a loud warning noise.

Meerkats make a special sound when they begin guard duty to let others know they're on the lookout.

Meerkats have many predators, including eagles, falcons, and jackals. To keep safe, meerkats dig special tunnels with wide openings, called bolt holes, throughout their territory. If danger is near, several meerkats can hide in the closest bolt hole together.

CRITTER COOPERATION

As long as there's no danger in the area, a sentry will make a quiet peeping noise. This continuous peeping is called the "watchman's song."

TERRITORIAL CRITTERS

The territory of one meerkat mob will often overlap the territory of another. This can be a problem because meerkats are very **territorial**.

Meerkats in two mobs that meet will line up and charge at each other. Mob members hold their tail out straight, kick out their legs, bend their back, and hiss to try to look scary. If one of the mobs doesn't back down, a deadly fight may break out. However, even though they're territorial, meerkats will sometimes allow an outsider to join their mob.

GLOSSARY

adaptation: A change in a living thing that helps it live better in its habitat.

burrow: A hole an animal digs in the ground for shelter.

dominant: In charge.

environment: The conditions that surround a living thing and affect the way it lives.

glare: Painfully bright sunlight.

growl: A deep, often angry sound.

mammal: Any warm-blooded animal whose babies drink milk and whose body is covered with hair or fur.

membrane: A soft, thin layer of matter that's part of a plant or animal.

protection: The act of keeping something safe from harm.

territorial: Used to describe animals that try to keep others away from an area they use or control.

venomous: Having a poisonous bite or sting.

whistle: A loud, clear sound.

INDEX

WEBSITES

Due to the changing nature of Internet links, PowerKids Press has developed an online list
of websites related to the subject of this book. This site is updated regularly. Please use this
link to access the list: www.powerkidslinks.com/atw/meer

24